CREATIVE

FLOWER ARRANGING

Text and Floral Designs: Jane Newdick
Photography: Steve Tanner, Neil Sutherland
Editorial: Laura Potts
Editorial Assistance: Janice Seymour
Design: Lindsey Philpott and Natasha Waters, Art of Design

CHARTWELL BOOKS
A division of Book Sales, Inc.
POST OFFICE BOX 7100
114 Northfield Avenue
Edison, N.J. 08818-7100

CLB 3360
© 1995 CLB Publishing, Godalming, Surrey,
U.K.
Printed and bound in Singapore
ISBN 0-7858-0345-9

CREATIVE

FLOWER ARRANGING

CHARTWELL
BOOKS, INC.

Introduction

$\mathcal{T}$here are many components that go to make a good arrangement. Certainly the choice of flowers and foliage is fundamental, yet even with a good selection of flowers and a carefully planned colour scheme an arrangement can so easily be spoiled.

The right container is a key part of the arrangement and it is important to choose one that will complement your display. Keen flower arrangers are always on the lookout for suitable containers and often second-hand shops and junk markets prove to be fruitful hunting grounds. Pretty china cups, jugs or dishes can be very useful and any small chips or cracks can be covered up with foliage or flowers. Some very basic types of vase, such as a shallow glass trough and a clear glass bowl, are very useful.

Keeping the arrangement in proportion is very important, as a display that is top heavy or unbalanced will never work well. As a general rule of thumb in a vertical arrangement the vase should be one third the total size of the arrangement and the overall effect should neither be top heavy or too sparse.

It is also worth bearing in mind that a knowledge of colour theory and styling will just give you a basis from which to work.

The rules are not hard and fast and you should not to feel constrained by them. Indeed, often some of the most interesting and successful arrangements seem to break all the rules.

This book is full of imaginative ideas for arranging flowers and gives clear, practical advice on how to create simple, yet stunning arrangements. It explains, with the aid of detailed step-by-step instructions, some of the techniques that are commonly used, giving you the confidence to tackle more complex formal displays. Whatever your knowledge of flower arranging, this compact, beautifully-illustrated guide helps you to explore the wonder of flowers, enabling you to use them to bring warmth and beauty to your home.

Getting Started

Before beginning it is important to choose the right tools. A pair of secateurs to cut woody stems and a pair of scissors to cut green stems are almost indispensable. For the keen flower arranger it might be worthwhile investing in a pair of florist's scissors. These have short, wide blades with blunt ends and lightweight handles and are ideal for nipping out the small leaves or stems from plants that are growing together.

A small knife to cut or pare stems without crushing them is also useful. Although specialist knives are available an ordinary kitchen knife will do just as well.

Floral foam to hold flowers in container arrangements is vital. The foam is available in different sizes of rectangular blocks and can be cut to shape, though some shapes are available in pre-cut form. It is important not to make the foam too wet as it can become crumbly and break off into pieces.

Chicken wire is used in heavier arrangements to give plants more support. It is also used in creating an arrangement in a narrow necked vase or one that is inwardly curving.

Finally, you will need wire and florist's tape. The wire is used to support flowers that have weak stems or heavy flower heads and the tape helps to disguise this wire in a display.

Conditioning Flowers

Time spent preparing fresh flowers prior to arranging them will be amply repaid, with individual blooms lasting longer and remaining more colourful for a longer period of time. It is probable that flowers that have been bought from a florists or a good market stall will have been conditioned. This is to say that the lower leaves will have been removed, the stems cut on a slant – so exposing a larger surface area – and the flowers left standing in water. Even so, to get the very best results it is probably a good idea to re-cut the stems and to let the blooms stand in water, even if it is only for a couple of hours. If, however, you buy a bunch of flowers out of water or if you pick them fresh from the garden then you will have to do all the conditioning yourself.

It is important to prepare flowers in this way as once submerged in water it is likely that any unremoved foliage will rot, making the water go cloudy and smell unpleasant. In addition, conditioning will ensure that the flowers are at their best when they are arranged and will retain their freshness for a longer period of time, prolonging the life of the display.

There are some plants that need more careful attention than others. Poppies, poinsettias and members of the Euphorbia family for instance have milky stems that need to be sealed. To do this use a match to singe the end. Others flowers, like delphiniums and lupins, have hollow stems that need to be filled with water and then plugged with cotton wool plug to ensure that water reaches the flower head.

Many of the plants used as foliage in arrangements have long woody stems, which are covered in bark. These need to have a different treatment from that for soft-stemmed annual or herbaceous flowers described above. Firstly the base of the stems should be cut on a slant and then a little of the bark stripped away. Then stem should then either be split by cutting a few slices upwards with sharp secateurs or a gardening knife, or by hammering the bottom few centimetres with a light mallet. Other pieces of foliage are better if they are fully submerged in water. To do this submerge them in a bath overnight.

Simple Arrangements

*O*ften the simplest arrangements can be the most effective. Flowers of a single variety can be arranged without any extra material to give maximum impact. In arrangements like this, it is vital that there appears to be a mass of flowers. If you only have a few flowers then use a smaller container in order to create this illusion.

Daffodils

Bright, cheerful daffodils have been cut to the same length and arranged in an oblong glass tank, with the flower heads only a little above the level of the container, to create a colourful early spring arrangement.

Instructions

Begin by filling the tank with water. Then take all the flowers in your hand and using a pair of scissors cut off the bottom of the stems to make them an equal length. With all the flowers in one hand, or both if the stems are very thick, put them into the tank, making sure that all the stems are touching the bottom. If the flower heads are very tightly packed together then loosen them out slightly.

Gerbera Daisies

This little arrangement of mixed gerberas is effective because it uses a mass of colour and texture to give the appearance of luxurious extravagance. The clever choice of container, an inexpensive shiny cake tin, adds to the arrangement, reflecting the colours of the flowers.

Instructions

Put a damp piece of florist's foam inside a container to hold the flowers in place. Cut the stems of the flowers quite short and push them into the foam, covering the whole surface and mixing the colours evenly.

Simple Arrangements

*S*trong in shape and colour, tulips are many people's favourite spring flower. They can, however, be difficult to arrange, as once they are in water they often bend and grow towards a light source. To strengthen the stems, wrap the flowers tightly in paper and stand them in water overnight.

Tulips

Tulips are available in a wide selection of brilliant colours and make stylish arrangements. It is important to try to find a container or vase that will complement the colour of the blooms. Here pale apricot tulips have been arranged in a contrasting green jug.

Instructions

Fill the vase with water and begin to arrange the conditioned flowers, ensuring that their stems are interlocking. For the most successful results choose a vase that is roughly one third of the height of the flowers. Once in water the tulips will find their own form.

Tulips and Roses

Tulips are versatile flowers that make good mixers, and work well with many other spring flowers. Here they have been combined with roses and ranunculus to make an eye-catching display.

Instructions

Remove all but a few of the leaves from the tulips. Fill a plain glass globe with water and begin the arrangement by interlocking the stems of the tulips to ensure that they remain in place. The flowers will find their own form, with the stems curving to make interesting shapes. Add the ranunculus and rose buds to give a good, solid contrast and to add height and body to the arrangement. If more foliage is needed add a few more of the tulip leaves.

Simple Arrangements

*O*ften the smallest posy of flowers can fill a room with scent. These easy arrangements use blooms that are as much a delight for their perfume as for their beauty.

Lilies

A few scented lily blooms have been arranged in a glass jelly mould with a selection of complementary flowers.

Instructions

To prepare the lily flower heads cut the stems quite short and give them a long drink in cold water. Choose a small, but relatively high-sided, vase or container and fill it with water. Place one lily head at the side of the container and then add the rest of the lilies one by one, working from one side of the container to the other. Finally, add the other extra flowers you are using.

Freesias

Freesias are noted for their lovely scent and though they come into season in the summer, they are usually available all the year round from florists.

Instructions

Fill the container with water and arrange the freesias, interlocking their stems. A good tip to keep the buds opening along the stem is to nip off the dried and faded flowers.

Simple Arrangements

*T*his celebration of summer flowers appears to break all the rules regarding colour and colour matching. Yet sometimes the most daring colour combinations are the most successful.

Garden Flowers

Here a selection of hot colours, including pinks, reds and oranges, have been combined to make a vibrant and eye-catching arrangement. Among the flowers used are poppies, schizanthus, honeysuckle, double buttercups and thrift.

Instructions

Pick and prepare a bunch of mixed garden flowers. If you have included poppies in your selection it is important to prepare them before beginning by holding each stem over a flame for a few seconds or by standing them in a shallow depth of boiling water for a few minutes. This seals the end of the stem and so helps to prevent the petals drooping or dropping. Cut the stems of the remaining flowers. Then, beginning at one side of a water-filled glass tank, put the flowers in place with the blooms facing towards the front. It is important to ensure that you mix both colours and types. Continue until all the flowers have been used up and you have a solid mass of blooms.

Clever Containers

*K*een flower arrangers are always on the look-out for interesting containers and vases and, as long as there is a way to line them or to conceal a container with water inside, the most unlikely containers can be pressed into service.

Violas and Pansies

Violas and pansies have been arranged in a mahogany tea caddy, in which a small jar of water has been hidden.

Instructions
Begin by carefully lining the box with a piece of plastic, then place the water-filled container in which you are to arrange the flowers inside. Trim the stems of the flowers to the length that you require and arrange them in the water. Flowers with shorter stems should be placed at the front.

Anemones

Silver can provide the perfect foil for the deep, velvety petals of a bunch of mixed anemones. Here they have been arranged in a silver cornucopia and have been offset by a smaller arrangement at its side.

Instructions

If the container in which you are to place the arrangement needs waterproofing, fit a watertight container into its neck. For an arrangement like the one in the silver cornucopia it is important that the stems are kept quite long, allowing the flowers to spill out over the top. Make sure that the heads of the flowers are left quite loose. For the arrangement in the lower dish, trim the stems very short. It is vital to choose a container of the right size, as this will give the illusion of plenty even if only a few flowers are used.

Clever Containers

*O*ften informal masses of flowers look best in a jug or simple container. These lively, fresh arrangements, though they look very impressive, are in fact quite easy to put together as all the stems are self-supporting.

Peach Roses and Bluebells

Pale peach roses and bluebells mixed with Queen Anne's lace have been used along with early beech foliage to give a light, airy arrangement, typical of spring.

Instructions

Begin by filling a vase with water. Put the conditioned stems of beech and Queen Anne's lace in place, spreading them out evenly through the arrangement. The vase will need to be quite full in order to hold the blooms in place. Next add the bluebell stems, arranging them throughout the foliage and aiming for a full but even effect. Add the roses and spray carnations with the blooms facing forward, using them to give depth to the arrangement.

Aquilegias and Cornflowers

This arrangement demonstrates how important the choice of vase is to the overall look of a display. The blues, mauves and purples of the flowers in this display mirror the colours in the pattern decorating the jug, creating an effective and unified whole.

Instructions

Choose a patterned container that is roughly one third to the height of the flowers and fill it with water. Choose a selection of flowers that complement this pattern and construct an open, lightly curved display.

Basic Shapes

*O*nce the basic techniques for constructing the all-round and fan-shaped arrangements illustrated here has been mastered, the principals can be applied to any number of different arrangements.

Roses and Carnations

This beautiful arrangement using sugar-pink roses and paler pink spray carnations is what is known as an all-round arrangement, designed to be seen from all angles. Though not particularly difficult to construct, the arrangement is very effective, being sophisticated without appearing artificial.

Instructions
Begin by choosing a low, wide-rimmed container and put damp foam or crumpled wire inside it. Stick the eucalyptus leaves in all over, making sure that they are firmly in place. The foliage should be used to construct the

basic, dome-shaped outline of the arrangement. For maximum effect and to ensure that the arrangement appears balanced, a few pieces of foliage should be left hanging down below the rim of the container. Next add the spray carnations, placing them evenly throughout the foliage and working all round the bowl. Finish by adding all the roses, filling the spaces and making a curved outline to the top of the arrangement.

White Honesty and Tulips

Here, white honesty is put with white tulips in a classical vase to create a light, fresh arrangement that complements dark surroundings perfectly.

Instructions

An arrangement like this may be top-heavy, a problem that it is best to counteract by fitting a square of crumpled wire mesh over a piece of damp foam positioned in the neck of the vase. The mesh, which should be convex and sit slightly higher than the neck of the vase, will help to keep the stems in place and held securely. Begin by pushing the stems of the tulips through the wire mesh, using them to create a gently rounded fan shape. Then add the white honesty or the other filler blooms, using them to flesh out the basic shape. To give greater depth to the arrangement, add a little dark green foliage, where it is needed to contrast with the individual blooms.

Basic Shapes

*F*oliage is often used in flower arranging to create the basic outline of an arrangement, and getting this right is often the key to the success.

Hyacinth and Ranunculus

Daffodils, ranunculus, hyacinths and genista have been combined to make a pretty and sweetly scented spring arrangement, that will charm visitors.

Instructions

Fill a small, round bowl with damp foam. Add spays of foliage and genista, starting with pieces to set the height and width of the arrangement and slowly building up the low, curved form that is its basis. Make sure that some sprays of foliage fall below the rim of the bowl. Spread the hyacinth heads and daffodils throughout the arrangement, using them to fill out the basic shape. Lastly add the ranunculus, mixing it in amongst everything else.

Dahlias and Coral Roses

This delightfully simple display uses an unusual combination of red, silver and lemon yellow flowers in a basic triangular-shaped arrangement. Scarlet dahlias and red roses are offset by tiny yellow santolina flowers and the soft green foliage of ballota and senecio.

Instructions

The secret of success in this arrangement lies in creating a strong basic outline with the foliage. Begin by packing a small, shallow bowl with damp foam, taping it into place if necessary, and then start to put the foliage in place. Start at the centre with quite a dense group of large leaves. Then use stems of ballota and senecio to create a triangular outline, making sure that pieces of foliage come below the rim of the container. Add the sprays of santolina with the flowers are facing forward, using it to fill out and soften the outline. Finally put the dahlias in place and then the rose stems, spacing them out well amongst the rest of the material.

Combining Colours

*T*oning yellows and oranges have been used in this display and illustrate well how the flower arranger can make use of basic colour theory to maximise the impact of an arrangement

Lemon Gerbera and Orange Lilies

Bright, sunny coloured ranunculus are mixed with lemon gerbera, orange lilies and pale lime green Viburnum Opulus to dazzling effect in this small, neat arrangement.

Instructions

Place a block of damp floral foam in a low vase and push the foliage and stems of viburnum firmly into it, to set the size and triangular shape of the display. Next add all the ranunculus, ensuring that it is spread evenly through the arrangement. Then add the lilies, placing them at the centre of the arrangement. Finally add the gerbera blooms, making sure that they are evenly spaced. It is important to condition the gerbera first by cutting the stems on a slant and putting the ends in a little boiling water. This will ensure that the ends are properly sealed and that the flowers will have a longer life in the arrangement.

Combining Colours

*T*hese colourful summer arrangements, though they use many of the same blooms, are very different in style and are a good illustration of how a flower arranger can create different moods.

Lilies and Ornamental Chillies

A mixture of ornamental chillies, alstroemeria, helichrysums, chrysanthemums and roses have been placed in a contrasting deep green jug. The flowers are offset perfectly by the soft silvery-grey eucalyptus foliage and the finished result is a natural-looking and unpretentious display.

Instructions

Fill the jug with water and add tall stems of yellow chillies and eucalyptus leaves to build a framework for the arrangement. Add the stems of alstroemeria, chrysanthemum and helichrysum, mixing them evenly among the foliage. Finally, add the roses, spreading them evenly around the jug to create a natural-looking display.

Lilies, Alstroemeria and Roses

Alstroemeria, chrysanthemums and roses have been combined with lilies and spray carnations in this late summer display. Foliage has been kept to a minimum, with the blooms providing all the texture and colour.

Instructions

Tape a block of damp florist's foam onto a shallow container and begin by positioning the opened lilies and the lily buds in it. It is important to keep the stems fairly short so that they sit low in the arrangement. Then add the chrysanthemums and roses balancing them carefully with the lilies. Use the alstroemeria and the spray carnations to add body to the arrangement and to fill any gaps. Finally, insert small branches of rosehip into the foam at intervals, using them to bring extra spice to the colour scheme and to give definition to the arrangement.

Beautiful Baskets

Baskets are almost tailor-made for arranging flowers. They provide a good background for almost all flowers and foliage, giving a pretty and natural look to arrangements.

Hyacinth Basket

This simple spring arrangement of pink and white hyacinths with deep evergreen foliage sets off the pretty basket to perfection.

Instructions

Place a large block of damp florist's foam in the lined basket, making sure that it fits snugly. Cover the foam all over with sprays of ivy, being careful not to cover the handle. The foliage should be used to emphasise the shape of the basket, with long pieces of foliage used to elongate the ends and with smaller, shorter pieces used to soften the sides. Put a mixture of pink and white hyacinth stems throughout the ivy, making sure that they are spread evenly through the arrangement. To get the best from this arrangement, keep it in a cool place, as hyacinths last longer this way.

Spring Basket

Hyacinths have been combined with ranunculus, freesia and narcissi in an unstructured way to create a colourful and fragrant spring display.

Instructions

Put a block of damp foam in the lined basket. Cover with bold, dark green foliage, creating a low, rounded shape and bringing some of the leaves over the sides of the basket. Then add the stems of hyacinth, making sure that they are spread evenly throughout the foliage. Use stems of freesia and ranunculus to soften the effect and to fill any gaps. To achieve the right effect, let a few stems curve downwards over the edge of the basket.

Beautiful Baskets

Country-Style Basket

Cream stocks, white honesty, honeysuckle, cream roses, alstroemeria and spray carnations have been arranged in a low basket to create a display that captures the essence of a British summer. The use of unusual foliage, which has been taken both from the hedgerow and the garden, gives the display a rich, old-fashioned, country house feel.

Instructions

A structured arrangement like this, which uses so much foliage and so many blooms, needs to be properly supported and time taken in preparation will pay dividends in the finished result. Line a low, rectangular basket with plastic or foil and then attach a lightweight plastic pin holder to the bottom. Use this pin holder to secure a large block of damp florist's foam firmly to the base of the basket. Then take a large piece of crumpled chicken wire and place it over the foam, making sure that it is attached to the sides of the basket. Begin to set the outline shape of the arrangement with foliage, pushing the stems through the crumpled chicken wire right into the foam. Add the long stems of stocks in a fan shape, with one facing forward at each side of the arrangement. Add the roses, carnations, honeysuckle and alstroemeria, mixing them well throughout the arrangement.

Gifts

*F*lowers have long been a symbol of love and when they have been chosen and arranged carefully they make a delightful gift.

Iris in Basket

Iris reticulata, bought as small pot plants, have been replanted into the lined basket, making a simple, yet beautiful gift.

Instructions

Use a basket that is already lined, or else line one with a strong piece of plastic. Loosen the soil around the edges of the pots and gently remove the plants. Put several into the basket, packing them quite close together. Fill any gaps with a little potting compost. Then use moss to cover this completely, fitting it around the stems of the plants.

Heart-Shaped Basket

Small, delicate summer flowers in a variety of complementary colours have been used to great effect in this little heart-shaped basket. Aquilegias have been combined with saxifrage, pelargonium flowers, mauve chive blooms and anemones.

Instructions

Cut a heart-shaped piece of foam to fit closely into the lined basket, then soak it and pack it into place. Starting at one end, begin pushing the stems into the foam, using a variety of flowers and making sure that they are packed closely together. Work across the basket, allowing some flowers to hang slightly over the edges. The overall effect should be of lush extravagance.

Gifts

A posy is one of the simplest ways to arrange flowers and, if it is done well, can be stood in water as a ready-made arrangement. Reminiscent of times long past, posies make an ideal gift.

Spring Posy

This delightful spring posy combines all the fresh colours of the season. Blue grape hyacinth are mixed with pale yellow primroses, wallflowers, sweet violets, white pulmonaria flowers and fresh green foliage.

Instructions

Begin with the central flower, in this case a sprig of wallflowers. Add a couple of grape hyacinths and a little foliage, holding the posy in your hand and working round it to make sure that the effect is even. Add primroses and other small flowers, mixing in more leaves as you go. To ensure that the posy takes on the traditional domed shape it is important to position each consecutive circle of flowers slightly lower than the preceding one. Finally, use a doily to make a paper collar to wrap around the posy. Ensure that the stems are tightly secured.

Garlands and Wreaths

Colourful wreaths and garlands make the most of seasonal flowers, providing colourful and welcoming displays. Though they may take time and a little patience to make, they are well worth the effort.

Summer Garland

Summer is the time of year that nature uses the brightest and strongest colours in her palette. Clematis, marigolds, roses, geraniums, sweet peas, geums and nasturtiums have been combined in this vibrant garland to make a colourful summer display.

Instructions

Begin by wiring some dry sphagnum moss to a wire wreath frame. Fill the frame with handfuls of moss, packing it tightly and securing it firmly with thin rose wire as you go along. Once all the frame is covered, spray the moss with water, until it is wet to the touch. Then begin to add the flowers and leaves, pushing the stems into the moss. It may be necessary to wire some of them secure. Work around the frame until it is completely covered and finish by spraying the finished garland with a mist of water to keep it fresh. Alternatively begin by covering the frame completely with leaves or filler material. Then add single flowers of the same type at regular intervals right around the frame.

Daisies, jasmine, feverfew, cornflowers, variegated mint leaves, love-in-a-mist and golden yellow achillea have been combined to make a fresh, *colourful garland. Strong colours like these always look good if they are mixed with plenty of white, as this provides a contrast.*

Garlands and Wreaths

*T*his beautiful evergreen wreath, decorated with white candles and silver baubles, makes an elegant Christmas display, full of festive cheer.

Christmas Wreath

This traditional circular Christmas wreath is made up of evergreen foliage and is decorated simply with a few small white candles and silver baubles. Like the summer garlands it is worked on a moss covered wire frame.

Instructions

This delightful Christmas wreath is simple yet effective. Like the Summer Garland (previous page) it is constructed on a moss covered wire frame. It is, however, a little more difficult to make, as the thicker stems of the evergreen foliage are not as easy to work with. Begin at the top of the frame and work around it using conditioned foliage. Try to use many different types of foliage, including variegated ivy, using it to build up an interesting pattern of colour in the wreath. Place the wreath on a large tray or low container and then decorate with the candles and baubles.

Conditioning Guide

A concise guide to preparing fresh flowers.

Alstroemeria
Cut stems and stand in water for a few hours.

Aquilegia
Cut stems and stand in deep water for a few hours.

Anemone
Dip ends in boiling water to seal, then stand in water.

Bluebell
Cut stems and stand in deep water for a few hours.

Broom
Crush stems and stand in water for a few hours.

Carnation
Cut stems and stand in water for a few hours.

Chrysanthemum
Crush stems and stand in water for a few hours.

Cornflower
Cut stems and stand in water for a few hours.

Daffodil
Cut stems on a slant and stand in water.

Dahlia
Fill stems with cold water and plug ends.

Freesia
Cut stems and stand in cool water for a few hours.

Geranium
Cut stems and stand in deep water for a few hours.

Gerbera
Dip ends in boiling water to seal, then stand in water.

Geum
Dip ends in boiling water to seal, then stand in water.

Grape hyacinth
Cut stems and stand in cool water.

Helichrysum
Cut stems and stand in water for a few hours.

Honesty
Cut the stems and stand in deep water for a few hours.

Honeysuckle
Cut stems and stand in deep water overnight.

Hyacinth
Cut stems, wrap tightly in paper and stand in water.

Lily
Cut stems and stand in cold water for a few hours.

Marigold
Cut stems and stand in cool water.

Narcissus
Cut stems and stand in cool water for a few hours.

Nasturtium
Cut stems and stand in water for a few hours.

Pansy
Cut stems and stand in water for a few hours.

Poppy
Seal end of stems with a flame, searing until black.

Primrose
Cut stems and stand in water for a few hours.

Queen Anne's lace
Dip ends in boiling water to seal, then stand in water.

Ranunculus
Cut stems and stand in deep water for a few hours.

Rose
Crush stems and stand in warm water.

Stock
Crush stems and stand in water for a few hours.

Sweet pea
Trim stems tand in deep water for a few hours.

Thrift
Cut stems and stand in deep water for a few hours.

Tulip
Wrap stems tightly in paper and stand in water.

Viola
Cut stems and stand in deep water for a few hours.

Violet
Cut stems and stand in cool shallow water.

Wallflower
Crush stems and stand in deep water for a few hours.